This book is intended to be used by a licensed clinician who is experienced in treating children and adolescents with gender identity challenges. The book is recommended for children 13 years old and older. The therapist should carefully screen patients to ensure that the child is at the developmental level to use the materials in the book. While all of the materials in the book may be appropriate for an individual 13-year-old, only selected few materials may be appropriate for another child of the same age. The therapist should therefore take into consideration a child's exposure and experiences in relation to the topic.

The workbook is written in simple language so that most children will understand. The activities are simple, yet have the potential of eliciting a lot of dialogue between the therapist and the patient. The therapist should ask a lot of open-ended questions to the patient's written responses.

Please refrain from asking "why" questions because the patient may feel like he or she needs to defend him or herself.

For questions or help using the workbook, I can be reached at hughalexis@yahoo.com.

Written by Hugh Alexis, MSW, LCSW-C
Edited by James Stimson
Illustrated by Lauren Bauman

In the box below, draw a picture of what you look like.

What do you like about how you look?

_____

_____

_____

What would you like to change about how you look?

_____

_____

_____

If you were to switch or change a body part, which body part would you switch or change? Explain.

_____

_____

_____

In the box below, draw a picture how you would like to look.

What do you like about this look?

_____
_____
_____

What don't you like about this look?

_____
_____
_____

What might other people not like about this look?

_____
_____
_____

How would you react to others who may not like this look?

_____
_____
_____

Jennifer's Story

Jennifer is a 14-year-old white female. She has been engaged in therapy since she was 6 years old because she experienced severe behavioral problems at home, school, and in the community. Recently, she shared with her therapist that she feels like she is attracted to girls. She claims that lately she has been thinking a lot about a particular girl in her class, whom she is attracted to. She reports that last week in her sex education class, the teacher asked the students to be honest about their sexuality. She further reports that students in the class were asked about their sexual preference. Furthermore, she reports that when she was asked about her sexual preference she responded to the teacher by saying; "My sexual preference is a question mark."

Have you ever experienced some of the feelings Jennifer shared? Yes   No

What feelings have you experienced? Explain.

_____

_____

_____

_____

Jennifer says that her sexuality is a question mark. In your opinion, what does Jennifer mean by that statement?

_____

_____

_____

_____

If you were to ask Jennifer a question, what would that question be?

_____

_____

_____

_____

Write a letter to Jennifer telling her how you feel about her story. Tell her about your own feelings and experiences about your sexuality. Tell her about your reactions to her story. Tell her what you like or didn't like about her story. Finally give her any suggestions you may have.

Dear Jennifer,

_____
_____
_____
_____
_____
_____
_____
_____
_____
_____
_____
_____
_____
_____
_____
_____
_____
_____
_____
_____
_____
_____
_____
_____

Richard's Story

Richard is a 16-year-old African American boy. He is extremely involved in football, basketball, track and field, and other sporting activities at school. Richard is very masculine and a lot of females at school are attracted to him. During his most recent therapy session, he told the therapist that he has something extremely private to share. He requested that the therapist refrain from sharing the information with his parents. Richard shared that he was attracted to males, and claims that two weeks ago he and Romeo kissed each other while they were walking home from school. He reports that after that interaction with Romeo, he has been thinking about Romeo a lot. He claims that he mainly thinks about Romeo at nights before he falls asleep.

Does Richard's story surprise you?   Yes   No

What did you find surprising or not surprising about Richard's story?

_____

_____

_____

_____

Richard specifically asked the therapist to refrain from sharing his story with his parents. What may be his reason for making this request?

_____

_____

_____

_____

If you were to say something to Richard's parents, what would you have said?

_____

_____

_____

_____

Animals

What is your favorite animal?

_____

In the box below, draw a picture of your favorite animal.

[ ]

How does this animal remind you of your sexuality? Explain.

_____

_____

What about this animal can you identify with? Explain.

_____

_____

Here is a list of animals you can choose from: bird, snake, cat, tiger, giraffe, pig, horse, goat, and sheep.

Pro-Social Activities

A pro-social activity is a positive activity which does not include negative behaviors.

What is your favorite indoor or outdoor pro-social activity?

_____

_____

In the box below, draw a picture of you doing your favorite pro-social activity. You may want to choose from the list below or you can come up with your own activity. Here is a list of some pro-social activities: running, jumping, skipping, dancing, basketball, football, swimming, wrestling, reading, and singing.

What do you like about this activity?

_____

_____

_____

_____

_____

Is there something about this activity that others may not want you to engage in?

_____

_____

_____

_____

_____

Has anyone ever condemned you for engaging in this activity?

Yes   No   Maybe

Explain what happened or what was said.

_____

_____

_____

_____

_____

If Yes, explain what that felt like.

_____

_____

_____

_____

_____

Colors

What is your favorite color?

_____

What do you like about this color?

_____

_____

_____

How does this color help define who you are or your sexuality?

_____

_____

_____

Choose one of the objects below and paint it with your favorite color.

What made you choose the object you chose? Explain.

_____

_____

Sex and Gender Terminologies

Do you remember Jennifer's experience earlier in the workbook? Jennifer was asked in class about her sexual preference and she reported that her sexuality is a question mark. Here are the responses of other students in Jennifer's class.

Juan says he is gay. Explain what that means to you.

_____

_____

Travis says he is bisexual. Explain what that means to you.

_____

_____

Linda says she is asexual. Explain what that means to you.

_____

_____

Olivia says she is straight. Explain what that means to you.

_____

_____

Antonio says he is homosexual. Explain what that means to you.

_____

_____

Trinity says she is pansexual. Explain what that means to you.

_____

_____

Gary says he is heterosexual. Explain what that means to you.

_____

_____

More Terminologies

Jennifer's teacher shared stories in class about other people whose sexuality are different. Explain what the terms below mean to you.

Celibate:

_____
_____
_____

Is this good or bad? Explain.

_____
_____
_____

Transgender:

_____
_____
_____

Is this good or bad? Explain.

_____
_____
_____

Metrosexual:

_____
_____
_____

Is this good or bad? Explain.

_____
_____
_____

Celebrities and Homosexuality

Find a socially acceptable picture of a celebrity who is gender non-conforming, gay, lesbian, transgender, or transsexual. You may find pictures online, in a magazine, or a newspaper.

Cut the picture and place it in the box below.

What about this celebrity do you admire?

_____

_____

_____

_____

What about this celebrity, if anything, do you not admire?

_____

_____

_____

_____

What is this person famous for?

_____

_____

_____

_____

If you could change one thing about this celebrity, what would it be?

_____

_____

_____

_____

What have you learned about this person that gives you hope or a lack of hope about your own sexuality?

_____

_____

_____

_____

People's Reactions to Gender Non-Conforming Children and Adolescents

Yesterday during lunch break, you overheard this conversation between Joan and Mary:

What were you thinking?

_____
_____
_____
_____
_____
_____

More Reactions to Gender Non-Conforming Children and Teenagers

Today you overheard this conversation between Greg and Sonya:

> Melissa told me that she is gay.
> Some of the kids are mean to her.
> I think she is a nice person.
> My mother says people do not choose to be gay,
> so Melissa should be proud of who she is.

> Yes! I heard Melissa is gay, but it doesn't bother me.
>
> Everyone is different.
> We cannot all be the same.
> If we were all the same, this would be a super boring world to live in.

What were you thinking?

_____

_____

_____

_____

_____

_____

In the last two activities you overheard two conversations. One was between Joan and Mary and the other was between Greg and Sonya.

Read both conversations again. Then write a letter to your therapist about how different people may react differently to gender non-conforming youth.

Dear Therapist,

_____

_____

_____

_____

_____

_____

_____

_____

_____

_____

_____

_____

_____

_____

_____

_____

_____

_____

_____

_____

_____

_____

_____

_____

_____

Experience in the family

Has anyone in your family made positive comments to you about your sexuality or who you are as a person? Yes   No

Who in your family has made positive comments or remarks to you?

_____

What did this person say to you?

_____

_____

How did that comment make you feel about that person?

_____

_____

How did it make you feel about yourself?

_____

_____

Has anyone in your family made negative comments to you about your sexuality or who you are as a person? Yes   No

Who in your family made negative comments or remarks to you?

_____

What did this person say to you?

_____

_____

How did that comment make you feel about that person?

_____

_____

How did it make you feel about yourself?

_____

_____

Experiences at School

Has anyone at school made negative comments about your sexuality?

Yes   No

What did the person say?

_____

_____

_____

How did you feel after the person made this comment?

_____

_____

_____

Who made this comment to you at school?

_____

_____

_____

What do you think was this person's motive or intention for making the comment? Explain.

_____

_____

_____

What did you say, or wish you would have said, to this person?

_____

_____

_____

You may or may not have verbally responded to this person, what was the result of your response or reaction to this person? Explain

_____

_____

_____

Opposite Sex friends

Name someone from the opposite sex you like very much.

_____

What about this person do you like?

_____
_____
_____
_____

Have you presently or in the past felt any attraction to this person? Explain.

_____
_____
_____
_____

Does this opposite sex friend know about your sexuality? Explain.

_____
_____
_____
_____

What may be some of the consequences, if any, should this person be made aware of your sexuality?

_____
_____
_____
_____

True or False

All gay males are feminine.   True   False   Unsure

All gay females are masculine.   True   False   Unsure

Gay people usually want to have intimacy with everyone of the same sex.
True   False   Unsure

Being gay is a curse from God. True   False   Unsure

There are gay people in every country and every profession.
True   False   Unsure

One out of every 8 people is most likely gay.   True   False   Unsure

Some gay people are open about their sexuality.   True   False   Unsure

Some gay people are closeted and private about their sexuality.
True   False   Unsure

Some gay people feel isolated and rejected by others which sometimes
trigger them to commit suicide.   True   False   Unsure

If someone had a same sex experience in the past, then it means that the
person is gay.   True   False   Unsure

Growing up

How would you describe the family in which you were raised or are being raised? Stable/unstable. Explain.

_____

_____

_____

In your family, have you ever felt like something or someone was missing. Explain.

_____

_____

_____

Have you ever been touched inappropriately, molested or sexually abused at a younger age? Explain.

_____

_____

_____

If you were sexually abused or molested, have you shared that experience with anyone? Explain your reason for sharing or not sharing that experience.

_____

_____

_____

How old were you when you realized you were different from other same sex peers? Explain what made you feel different.

_____

_____

_____

Coming Out

Kieron is a 13-year-old African American male. He has been engaged in the therapeutic helping process for the past year due to his struggles with depression. Lately he shared with the therapist that he is sexually attracted to other males. Kieron reports that he has accepted his sexuality, and claims that he is okay with being gay. He claims that he wants to share his likeness to same sex peers with his parents, and states that he is fearful because they may no longer want to be his parents and that he may end up being homeless.

Tell Kieron why his decision may be good or bad. Explain.

_____

_____

_____

_____

Tell him what about his feelings or fears may be realistic, meaning that this fear can indeed happen. Explain.

_____

_____

_____

_____

Tell him what about his fears may be unrealistic, meaning this fear can never happen. Explain.

_____

_____

_____

_____

Looking Back

Earlier in the work book you overheard a conversation between Joan and Mary about Melissa.

Write a letter to Joan and Mary letting them know that Melissa's sexuality does not totally define who she is as a person since we all have other aspects of our personalities which in combination make us who we are. For example: caring, jovial, happy, considerate, intelligent, love and protect animals, love and protect people, generous, environmentally sensitive

Dear Joan and Mary,

_____
_____
_____
_____
_____
_____
_____
_____
_____
_____
_____
_____
_____
_____
_____
_____
_____
_____
_____
_____

Coping Strategies

Here are some cognitive messages you can say to yourself to cope with negative behaviors displayed by others, and negative comments others may have made towards you.

My sexuality is only one side of me.

My sexuality does not define who I am as a person.

I love myself for who I am and _____ loves me too.

My determination and ambition will define who I am.

Now come up with your own positive self-talk. You may want to write one on a piece of paper and read it before going to bed at nights. If you read it regularly, you will trick your brain into believing it.

1. _____
   _____
   _____
   _____
2. _____
   _____
   _____
   _____
3. _____
   _____
   _____
   _____

Sadness

What makes you most sad about your sexuality?

_____

_____

_____

_____

What time of the day do you experience the most sadness?

_____

_____

_____

_____

What makes the sadness worse?

_____

_____

_____

_____

What makes the sadness better?

_____

_____

_____

_____

If you were to use a magic wand to fix your problem, what would the wand do? Explain.

_____

_____

_____

_____

_____

_____

Happiness

You may be treated differently by others because of your sexual preference. This may cause you to feel sad, but some things may bring you happiness. List and explain two positive things which bring you happiness and two negative things which bring you happiness.

Positive thing:

_____
_____brings me happiness.

Explain.

_____
_____

Positive thing:

_____
_____brings me happiness.

Explain.

_____
_____

Negative thing:

_____
_____brings me happiness.

Explain.

_____
_____

Negative thing:

_____
_____brings me happiness.

Explain.

_____
_____

Self-Harm and Suicide

Have you ever thought of injuring or killing yourself because of your sexual preference? Explain.

_____

_____

_____

_____

_____

When did you first experience this thought? Explain.

_____

_____

_____

_____

When was the last time you experienced this thought? Explain.

_____

_____

_____

_____

What did you contemplate doing? Explain.

_____

_____

_____

_____

What did you think about, if anything, that prevented you from carrying out this plan? Explain.

_____

_____

_____

_____

Safety Contract

If you are currently thinking of killing yourself, or have thought about it within the past 2 weeks, it is strongly recommended that your therapist do a safety contract with you. A safety contract is one way to ensure that you get the help you need instead of resorting to negative self-harming behaviors.

I _____ agree that I will not harm/kill myself. I agree that I will speak to a caring adult _____ if I am experiencing suicidal thoughts or other thoughts of hurting myself. If no one is available to talk to, I agree to call 911 immediately.

_____

_____

Therapist Signature / Date

_____

_____

Client Signature/ Date

Expressing yourself and your sexuality in a manner that reflects who you are, your perceptions, talents and skills.

Below is a picture of the international sign commonly used by the LGBT community.

Do you think this symbol is appropriate? Explain.

_____
_____
_____

What about this symbol do you like or not like? Explain.

_____
_____
_____

If you were to come up with your own symbol to represent your sexuality, what will that symbol be? Draw your symbol on the next page and feel free to use colors to bring out your own creativity.

What do you like about this symbol? Explain.

_____

_____

_____

_____

Future Concerns/Fears

Many gay teens experience concerns and sometimes fears about their future life. Some areas of future potential fears are listed below. Respond to the ones which you think may be a concern for you.

Having Children.

This is or isn't a concern for me because:

_____

_____

_____

_____

My Profession.

This is or isn't a concern for me because:

_____

_____

_____

_____

My Neighbors.

This is or isn't a concern for me because:

_____

_____

_____

_____

Now come up with a concern which wasn't mentioned in the work book.

_____

_____

This is a concern for me because:

_____

_____

_____

_____

Comparison

In the first activity you drew a picture of what you looked like. Now without looking back at the picture. Draw another picture of what you think you look like after completing all or most of the activities in the workbook. Your picture may change or it may have remained the same.

Your therapist will process the picture with you and provide feedback. The therapist may restate some of your comments, reframe some of your comments, confront some of your comments and he or she may validate some of your comments.

Final Project

Create a mini collage below which will capture what you want your future life to look like. You may use pictures from magazines, newspaper, or the internet. If you want to make a bigger collage you can do so. Bring the collage with you to your next session so that your therapist can process with you.